Mountaintops
and Molehills

Mountaintops and Molehills

Essays in Haphazard Theology

Tom Mullen

WORD BOOKS
PUBLISHER
WACO, TEXAS

MOUNTAINTOPS AND MOLEHILLS

ISBN 0-8499-2930-X
Library of Congress Catalog Card No: 80-53254

The Scripture quotation marked NEB is from *The New English
Bible*, © The Delegates of the Oxford University Press and The
Syndics of The Cambridge University Press, 1961, 1970; used by
permission. The quotation marked Phillips is from *The New
Testament in Modern English*, copyright © 1958, 1959, 1960 by
J. B. Phillips; used by permission of the MacMillan Company.
All other quotations are from the Revised Standard Version of
the Bible, copyrighted 1946, 1952, © 1971, 1973 by the Division
of Christian Education of the National Council of the Churches
of Christ in the U.S.A., and are used by permission.

To Alan, Keith
Miriam, Fred, Wil, Jim,
Leonard, Dick, Hugh,
Dee, Claudia, and Vern

Contents

Preface

  I.   Preview of Past Attractions.....................11

  II. Much Ado about *Some* Things 15
       Entering College   18
       Football Fervor   21
       Christmas Greetings!   25
       Family Reunions   27
       Animal House   30
       A Cottage by the Lake   33

  III. Songs for the Unsung 37
       On Committees   40
       On Vacation Church School   43
       On the Blessed Doorkeepers   46
       On Keeping the Nursery   49
       On Church Suppers   52
       On Sermons   56

  IV. Virtue Reconsidered 59
       Cowboys and Truckdrivers   62
       Hot Weather Lessons   65
       "Thanks, God—We Needed That"   68
       The "Good-Health" Gospel   71
       The Patience of Patients   74
       Let It Shine, Anyhow!   77

V.   Moments of Truth 81
   Ice Will Suffice 84
   Term Paper 102 87
   Strangers to Our Best Selves 90
   On Thinking about My Wife and Realizing That We've
    Been Married Over 25 Years and Are Going to Stay
    That Way 95
   Goin' Fishing 98

Preface

This book would not have been written except for the help and cooperation of others. Several persons, therefore, share the blame.

Bob Wersan wrote the poem, "At the Cinema," for the Earlham College library magazine, *The Crucible,* in 1956. It was just right for the chapter entitled "Cowboys and Truck-drivers." Thanks, Bob, wherever you are.

The chapter, "Strangers to Our Best Selves," is based on—nay, largely plagiarized from—a sermon given by Jim Yerkes, esteemed colleague at Earlham School of Religion. While almost all of the rest of the book is based on my own experience or observation, Jim's comments spoke with such truth that I appropriated them for a chapter. Next time, Jim, either copyright your material or be less profound.

Several chapters are based on articles which appeared in *The Disciple* magazine. Jim Merrell, the editor, is hereby thanked for allowing me to write a monthly column, "Mullin' It Over," since 1974, articles which often threatened the dignity and quality of the magazine.

Cheryl Fleagle typed the manuscript with skill and patience in spite of the several misspellings and marginal notes I provided to keep her alert. She deserves credit for correcting my corrected corrections correctly.

Two groups, however, merit special appreciation. We all live at the expense of others, and writing a book—even a small, insignificant one—is costly in both time and energy. When they are spent at the desk, they are not available to family and friends.

My wife, Nancy, understands this because she shares a dream. Besides, she is the subject of an entire chapter. Daughters Sarah and Martha, both college students, make fewer family claims now, so I probably missed time with them more than they missed it with me. Brett and Ruthie, however, made some sacrifices. We played softball, rode bikes, and swam together less often than we wanted. Now that the book is finished, we can return to important matters like these.

The other group, besides my family, which shared in the cost of this book's creation is made up of my colleagues at Earlham School of Religion. They often took my place and explained my absence. They tolerated my idiosyncrasies and endured the "haphazardness" of my work among them.

Thus, this book is dedicated to them—to Alan, Keith, Miriam, Fred, Wil, Jim, Leonard, Dick, Hugh, Dee, Claudia, and Vern. It is my way of saying "thanks," and is offered with sincerity, respect, love, and in place of a share in the royalties.

TOM MULLEN

I PREVIEW OF PAST ATTRACTIONS

In life, it would be easier to play our parts if we had a copy of the script. As it is, we are like amateur carpenters building a house: first we do it, then we learn how.

The special temptation of middle age is to think we've learned how. True, we *have* learned some things, but mostly we've acquired experience—which is not identical to knowing. Experience teaches us what fools we used to be, but not what fools we're going to be. We can learn from experience, but much of our time and energy is spent *recovering* from it. Experience has a way of giving the test first and the lesson later.

The problem with experience is that few are born with it. It comes only with age—which is when it does us the least good. After acquiring it, we feel an overwhelming desire to share it with others, most of whom would rather do it themselves. Teenagers in particular have concluded that a parent's experience is a poor teacher and a worse preacher. Sentences that begin, "When I was your age . . ." are as welcome as water to a drowning man. Wise parents, therefore, rather than speaking from experience, from experience, don't speak.

Still, we've accumulated the memorabilia of living forty-five or fifty years, and it's a shame to let it go to waste. We've progressed from confident ignorance to thoughtful uncertainty. We've acquired some clues as to how much is too much. We've discovered there are no answers to the problems of life in the back of the book, and whatever we've learned about making the most of life will have to be shared before most of it is gone.

Thus, middle age is a good time to pause for breath in the human race. We *make* some things happen in our lives, and we *watch* a lot of other things happen. But seldom do we figure out the meaning of what *has happened*. It's good, in other words, to take breaks from the action and become philosophers of life—more specifically, philosophers of *our* lives.

Not that others will necessarily extract Deep Meanings from our lives—from our molehills and mountaintops. However, they may be encouraged to reflect upon their own. If a middle-aged man, gray-headed, father of four children, husband of one wife (the last two, let us hasten to add, in reverse order) can find meaning in his ordinary life, others can do so, too.

Thoreau said: "My life is not an apology. It is a life." Every life has meaning. Not just the lives of people the media have made famous nor those who become saints, but ours, too, are important. A man attending a seminar for depressives was heard to say, "It's possible that my whole purpose in life is simply to serve as a warning to others." That's not much but it's something. Even better is the view of life articulated by

J. B. Phillips in his paraphrase of Matthew 5:5—"Happy are those who accept life and their own limitations. They will find more in life than anybody."

Those able to pause and reflect upon their lives at age forty-six will find many characteristics different from what they, at age twenty-one, expected. I, for example, once thought of myself as a budding intellectual. Years later I realize I am not. College professors do not assign my books as required reading. In fact, they don't assign them at all, and at best they give a copy to their grandmothers for Christmas. Intellectuals are supposed to like abstract art; I can't understand it. Professors are not supposed to enjoy *The Sound of Music;* I've seen it five times. Should I hear the *William Tell* Overture, I invariably think of the "Lone Ranger."

No matter. Let us use what brains we have and respect our limitations and we, too, may find more happiness than anyone.

Others may have foreseen themselves as models of Christian piety. In their youth they planned to imitate the lives of Great Christians about whom they had read. They spent hours each day on their knees in prayer. They read the Bible, even the "begats," without ceasing. And they always did so early in the morning before breakfast and usually before dawn's early light. That's how saints got to be saints.

So we, too, make periodic resolutions to be devotional—to start each day in prayer and to do so early. Along the way, however, most of these good intentions become part of the road to somewhere other than sainthood. Maybe saints have different body clocks, and probably they don't stay up for the eleven o'clock news. Whatever the differences, one day we come to terms with *our* own ways and means of cultivating the devotional life, and those terms may not be a model for any other Christian. Incidentally, the chapters in this book sometimes conclude with a prayer but often do not. Here, as in life, we don't always pray in traditional ways or by a regular schedule. Only unpredictability can be depended upon in the devotional life.

In fact, few of the experiences of life turn out the way they're supposed to turn out. Big events that are expected to be Meaningful, on which we've spent time, energy, and money and for which we've provided mood music in the background often fall flat.

Yet, just when we resign ourselves to living with dampened expectations, moments of truth, joy, or love burst unannounced into our experience. We look back on them, sometimes years later, and discover God's presence was there.

Life, therefore, is unlike a trip planned by a travel agency with every reservation made, each event carefully scheduled, and all unpleasantness screened out of sight. On the contrary, life is like a journey taken on our own recognizance with many spontaneous side trips and quite a few wrong turns. Some of us discover we occasionally read the map upside down, and often we like the new places we find so well we never go on to our original destination.

Christians are like the Israelites on the way to the Promised Land. We have some idea of *where* we want to arrive, but we don't know *when* and often we'd just as soon turn back. Our experiences of God are frequently different from what we'd expected and seldom complete, neat, and totally clear. About the time our experience verifies something we've believed with our heads or learned in Sunday School, another adventure sends us back to the drawing board. Only in seminary do we learn systematic theology. In life we experience haphazard theology.

There is no need, however, for self-pity. The joy of a pilgrimage is making the trip, detours and all. The Israelites were lost in the wilderness, attacked by their enemies, guilty of sins, and victims of their own stupidity. In many ways they were like real people. The one fact that made them special was that God was with them.

We, too, are real people. And God is with us.

II MUCH ADO ABOUT SOME THINGS

Most of us celebrate the obvious. It is difficult to overlook Christmas when Santa Claus arrives in October by helicopter at the shopping mall, and stores begin shopping-days countdown on December 1. Similarly, Thanksgiving, Easter, Memorial Day, and the Fourth of July are front and center in our consciousness, unless we recently arrived from outer space.

There are personal celebrations, too, we usually observe. Birthdays, anniversaries, and graduation parties are occasions we remember, and we had better have some fancy explanations ready if we don't. Much of the fun and laughter at such times is unplanned; for instance, a look at our wedding pictures twenty years later is guaranteed to provoke laughter from friends and near-hysteria from our children. Then, too,

15

many of us are reaching an age when we're not eager for more birthdays but can sure use the presents.

The need is for *more* celebrations, however, not fewer. One person we know occasionally sends bouquets to celebrate Monday. Mortgage-burning parties were once festive occasions back when it was possible to complete payments during a lifetime. The parents who spell "you're super!" with chocolate chips on a cake to celebrate a no-occasion day proclaim loudly they like their kids.

Most lump-in-the-throat occasions occur at times other than traditional ones. The addition of a guinea pig to the family menagerie was not an especially happy event for this writer, but the excitement and joy it generated for a ten-year-old was a moment of celebration. Getting excited when our team wins means more when we remember it's a game and not a war. Sending Christmas cards ranks with present wrapping as a seasonal party-pooper—until a special note to a special person rekindles a flame.

Many tears fill many eyes when one's child marches across a stage to receive a high school diploma. The occasion becomes less sentimental, however, when perspiration from the ninety-six degrees of the gymnasium mixes with the tears, and your child's name is one among four hundred and twelve graduates. However, when the same daughter begins college life three months later (in a coed dorm!), both you and she know that a new day has dawned. As was not true before that moment, she is in charge of her life.

Going to family reunions is an important gesture for some but an act of self-flagellation for others. Yet, when we go to a reunion under duress (translation: to please a spouse) and end up having an enjoyable time, banners should be flown, incense burned, and a private holiday declared.

Certain events, of course, are so private only one or two even know a celebration is occurring. No outward ritual is observed, and the quiet beating of the heart, a tiny smile, and a shared glance are the only marks of the significance of the occasion. Persons—like ministers—who have never owned a home, and who then one day are handed the keys to their (and a bank's) property will understand that special moment. Those who experience the ritual of hanging the family name over the door will be sharing a celebration.

Happy are they whose ability to rejoice is great. They will find much to celebrate.

Entering College

The arrival on campus of new students inspires mixed emotions.
Parents shed tears as their child embarks upon a significant
new adventure, and they inwardly rejoice at the prospect of
once again using the family car. The young men and women
tremble with excitement at being "on their own." They, of
course, are not yet experientially aware that a dean of
students, faculty advisers, dormitory counselors, and two
chaplains are standing by armed with assignments, regula-
tions, and expectations not unlike those established for
prisoners of war.

Faculty are also ambivalent in their reactions to each
entering class. While they delight in the prospect of fresh
tuition money to pay their salaries, they view new students as
a mixed blessing. Granted, many of the students arrive eager
for Truth, and all come unacquainted with a professor's old
lectures, which is one of the great differences between
teaching students and preaching to congregations. Faculty
also know that academic excellence is not always the primary
concern when students choose a college. Conscientious
teachers who have labored diligently over a hot curriculum to
produce interesting programs and integrative courses know
that only a few will drink deeply of the fountain of
knowledge. Many will only sip and most merely gargle.

Some students conscientiously avoid serious contact with
formal education while in college. Nonetheless, several

18

among this group manage to graduate, and are able to boast that they never took a class held above the first floor or before ten o'clock in the morning. These students know that a little learning is a dangerous thing, and many spend four years in complete safety.

Lots of students enter college eager to achieve certain goals, but these may have little to do with books or courses. There are, for example, some who select a college in the first place because of its opportunities for contacts. It is not what they know, but *who*, that is important. They rigorously avoid learning *how* to do things so that they will, therefore, *not* have to do them. Such students are attracted to universities with honor systems because they are willing to let the school have the honor so long as they can have the system. Many men and women in this category graduate and go on to become administrators and government officials.

A number of freshpersons bring romantic notions to college. Whatever else is acquired, the college years are deemed a success if a spouse is included. Sadly, not all college men and women are interested in permanent relationships, and many young people are therefore doomed to disappointment. As one woman student—not an English major—stated her feelings: "I came here to be went with, and I ain't been."

Most colleges attract a few persons who come expecting to study, do research, and glean information. Faculty members delight in such men and women because students whose interests are scholastic have a tendency to be set apart. They become the next generation of Ph.D.s, living evidence that the system works well enough at least to reproduce itself.

The media and the entertainment industry provide images of college life which accentuate the bizarre and highlight the grotesque. "Animal House" behavior is still more characteristic of a zoo than of a college, and excessive drinking is regarded as a problem, not a virtue, at most universities. Nevertheless, the combination of media-produced fantasies

19

and original sin causes sweaty palms for parents who are about to deposit their daughter or son on a campus for four years. Good, academic colleges are not coeducational nunneries, and that fact unnerves many middle-aged parents.

Thus, parents who send their children to institutions of higher learning are tempted to rush in with warnings and advice: "Study hard! Be good! Beware of smooth talking men! Beware of smooth talking women! Caution! When in doubt, don't!" The temptation is real because the pitfalls are real. A cynic might conclude that higher education is merely the process of changing blissful ignorance into some other kind of ignorance.

Which is why we do well to butt out. Let new students have their dreams and anticipations. College is *not* different from the real world. It is a microcosm of it. Within it are "Animal Houses" and "Ivory Towers." There are times of wholehearted horseplay and other Deep Moments. The people who attend them are strong and weak, faithful and unfaithful, enrolled for right reasons or no good reason. Just like Life.

As our sons and daughters enter college, we parents are well advised to settle for whatever Christian nurture has been absorbed to that point. Granted, Christian faculty need to be available to students—when *asked*. Neither concerned parents nor conscientious teachers, however, can be faithful *for* them, that is, *in their place*.

Fortunately, Christ has promised to be with us—and them—always, even to the end of the age. And that's a long time, even longer than a semester or the period between the letters our child neglects to write.

Football Fervor

The place of college football in American life is secure. Coaches of big university teams are often paid higher salaries than full professors, and the success or failure of the Team carries enormous financial considerations.

Many alumni vicariously relive their university days each Saturday during the season, and they don't like it when their team plays like a bunch of amateurs.

One besieged university president, it is rumored, identified the three main parts of his job as providing parking for the faculty, sex for the students, and football for the alumni.

Such a reaction, of course, is extreme, as faculty actually have few parking problems. There is no doubt, however, that college football fans are a special breed whose emotions and loyalties are comparable only to Japanese Kamikaze pilots in World War II. They care deeply about their team and will stand by the players and coaches, win or tie.

The reasons for their passion are several, but alumni connections are not the only factor. Religion, race, geography and lifestyle all play a part in determining which teams they support. One definition of an atheist, in fact, is a person who watches a Notre Dame–Southern Methodist game and doesn't care who wins.

Regional loyalties influence fan attitudes, too. People who did not attend the University of Michigan and may think Northwestern is located in Oregon will cheer for one or the other because of the Pennsylvania players on the team. The glory and honor of the great state of Ohio seemingly rests on the well-padded shoulders of the Buckeye football team, and the main reason so few of its fans commit suicide over the disgrace of losing is that it almost never does.

The effects of such fervor and dedication by alumni and other fans are not always positive. Some universities—usually those with poor records—worry about providing better education instead of better football. A few have adopted strict rules about academic requirements, refusing to grant a varsity letter to any athlete who cannot identify where it comes in the alphabet. (Football itself, as this former player knows, is an extremely complicated game, best appreciated by those smart enough to understand it and dumb enough to think it important.)

Others worry that the tremendous emphasis on winning breeds poor sportsmanship, as some players are good losers but others don't pretend. Fans and coaches are well-known for their fair-mindedness, too, and frequently offer helpful suggestions to referees and opponents about how to play the game and where to spend eternity.

Still, all things work for good with those who love the Lord, and football fans—as other sinners—experience both blessing and pain. They learn to rise above suffering—anyone who can sit for hours on a cold seat, eating peanuts, is no weakling. Former players replay their big games again and again, as nostalgia and the absence of eyewitnesses move them closer and closer to All-American each passing year.

Some merely enjoy the game, either as spectators or participants. They seem able to appreciate good plays in and of themselves, even those made by the Other Guys. They treat football as an enjoyable competitive event that has no cosmic significance. Such persons may be the saving remnant. For those who see football as a *game* are worth their weight in gold—or roughly the cost of two seats on the fifty yard line of the Michigan–Ohio State game.

Prayer: "O Great Scorer, help us to keep the fun in our games, even football, and even when we lose. In the name of him who couldn't be beaten. Amen."

Christmas Greetings!

Most Christmas card lists, psychologists point out, have three categories. First, there are the "reciprocals"—relatives, friends, and people who send a card to us because we sent one last year to them. Or did they originally send one to us and we sent one to them because they sent one to us? Whoever is to blame, many of us have people on our lists we wish would break the habit first.

The best reciprocals are those with short notes from good friends long time not seen. The worst are those without return addresses, signed "Affectionately, George and Helen"—when we can't remember whether it is *that* George and Helen or the ones we dropped off the list last year.

A second category are those greeting cards in the "send but not receive" group. Employers, benefactors, and those whose social status is coveted fall into this grouping. College presidents, business executives, and Distinguished Persons receive cards each year from persons who would very much like to be remembered during the Joyous Season and even more when the time for promotion arrives.

Those of us, of course, who would not think of sending cards for such reasons will probably mail a few to persons not on our regular list and from whom we do not expect a card in return. Our motives are pure, informed by the Christmas spirit, and only slightly influenced by the fact the recipients may remember they offered to lend us their speed boat at the lake next summer.

The third category, of course, is that of "receive but not send." It consists of people who want to borrow *our* boats and get on *our* lists. Banks, businesses, and others to whom we owe money are also in this category, and they send us greetings without expecting a reply but gently reminding us we had best not leave town.

The types of cards that we send also reveal Deeper Meanings. Museum prints with one's name embossed in gold show taste and usually come from a childhood friend best remembered for having glued the music teacher's piano keys together. UNICEF cards, baby photographs, or homemades are clues to our values and priorities. They are not always hard evidence, of course, as our card selections are frequently determined by what the Cub Scout troop was selling this year.

Mimeographed Christmas letters are sometimes warm and welcome documents, happily received and more valued than an expensive gift. At their worst, however, they reveal human vanity as obvious as a case of chicken pox. Their tone compares with that used in addressing a mental defective, and the content of the letter—sometimes three or four pages—tells us more and more about less and less until we know almost everything about practically nothing that interests us.

Often they are written in the third person, sometimes from the perspective of the family dog or pet cat, e.g., "While Herbert spent his time in Paris meeting local politicians and Dorothy languished in posh salons, I guarded the hotel room and flirted with a French poodle."

Alas! Such letters pose an important question: Are Christmas greetings sent for *bad* reasons better than no greetings at all?

We'll never know for sure, as motives have a way of

changing. A card sent out of indifference may be *received* with joy and thanksgiving. Certainly it is good spiritual discipline to examine our lists and reasons, even if we are among that rapidly dwindling percentage of Americans who can afford cards and the postage for sending them.

If we do so, most of us will discover selfish motives as well as sincere desires to communicate joy and love. We may find that we have more superficial relationships than we wished we had, but we may also learn how rich in affection and friendship we are. Who knows, too, they *may* remember to lend us their boat!

Best of all, examining our list may remind us that remembering others is the heart of Christmas. In one sense greetings and gifts are always reciprocal: we love because God in Christ first loved us. It was God—not Hallmark—who cared enough to send the Very Best.

Family Reunions

"A close relative" has come to mean one you see occasionally between funerals. Most American families—meaning the "clan" of grandparents, aunts, cousins, and in-laws covering several generations—do not live in proximity to one another. Given the mobility of our time, in fact, most relatives—even close ones—are distant.

Except at holidays. Either out of sentiment or custom, families will travel great distances in bad weather at considerable expense to see relatives they might fail to recognize on the street. True, some family members are *both* related to *and* genuinely fond of one another. Others are best appreciated when they deprive the rest of the family the pleasure of their company. And for certain clan members—the nephew who didn't succeed in business, the daughter-in-law who dropped out of college, or Uncle Charlie who drinks too much—Christmas reunions can be a fete worse than death.

This should not surprise us. Blood may be thicker than water, but it also boils at a lower temperature. Modern families are often extraordinarily diverse, having within them members who march to many different drummers. It is not uncommon to find within the same clan persons who have married across cultural boundaries, joined unusual religious sects, or learned to like yogurt. When they appear at the same house for a reunion, they more often resemble the United Nations at lunch than a family gathering.

At least, that's the way it is with this writer's family, and our experience may be typical of many other reunions.

When the clan gathers at Christmas, there is the mathematical probability that three generations, fifteen grandchildren, nine adults, and a partridge in a pear tree will show up. Among them will be Missouri Synod Lutherans, Quakers, Presbyterians, Disciples, a Jehovah's Witness, and a couple of evangelical pagans. At least two family members privately believe that to be a Democrat *and* a Christian is a contradiction in terms, yet since some of their own children have so strayed from the "right" way, they tend to emphasize the love and forgiveness of Almighty God.

Lifestyles of the various members of the clan often have less in common than those of Billy and Jimmy Carter. Some within the family feel that no celebration can properly be carried out without abundant portions of Christmas spirits. One grandmother, however, has long been active in the WCTU, and her teetotaling son-in-law has stated he would rather steal than take a drink—and has been so accused by other family members.

One uncle smokes cigars so noxious that his own sister has threatened to report him to the Environmental Protection Agency. The vegetarians in the group bring their own food in order to survive, and the veterans of foreign wars swap battle experiences while unwrapping the peace medallions their pacifist nieces gave them for Christmas.

Along with religious, political, and lifestyle differences are blended personal idiosyncrasies which would seem to eliminate any reasonable possibility that these people share bloodlines. The Ph.D. in Islamic history wants to discuss the Middle East crisis (he *always* wants to discuss the Middle East crisis!) while his sister prefers to lecture him on his family responsibilities. The hypochondriac pursues his brother-in-law/doctor, seeking free medical advice about itching hemorrhoids. The grandchildren sometimes choose up sides in order to leave someone out—which leads to familial peer group rivalry, a fancy name for one kid punching a cousin on the nose.

Given the intergenerational, cross-cultural, biracial, and ecumenical composition of the family, it is astounding that they bother to get together at all. Bordering on the miraculous, moreover, is the fact that the gatherings are mostly pleasant and full of good cheer.

Why? How does it happen? It happens when ties that bind are stronger than differences. The man who wasn't good enough to marry your daughter turns out to be the father of the best grandchildren in the world. Long-married people, when warned at crucial moments by a spouse's discouraging glare, learn to chuckle at bad jokes and congenital peculiarities. Grim-lipped determination to make the best of the event softens into warm-hearted congeniality.

All of which shows that the spirit of reconciliation Christmas fosters continues to work its miracle. At Christmas family gatherings we're not supposed to argue, and—doggone it!—we don't! The miracle is not unlike the one Isaiah prophesied: "The wolf shall dwell with the lamb, and the leopard shall lie down with the kid, and the calf and the lion and the fatling together, and a little child shall lead them" (Isa. 13:6).

At Christmas we may discover we love our relatives, and new hope for peace in the world is born.

Prayer: "O God, who brings people together, we ask your presence at reunions. Open our eyes to the virtues of relatives, particularly on the side of the family where they are most hidden. Grant the little children drowsiness, so that they might nap before dinner. In the name of him whose brothers and sisters are those who do your will. Amen."

Animal House

Background Information: The occasion for this essay was the solemn announcement that one of the guinea pigs, supposedly a male, was pregnant. The younger children were ecstatic and began laying plans for a baby pig shower. The author retired to his study and wrote this essay, doubtless a better response than his initial impulse—petitioning Congress to declare his home a wildlife preserve.

In China, we are told, pets have been abolished; this has saved lots of money, considerable time, and a great deal of street cleaning. Among our children, however, this information may inspire more loyalty to the United States of America than all the patriotic speeches ever given.

Children and animals go together. Young boys and dogs are much alike—creatures of impulse, irresponsible, and full of energy that seldom is harnessed to any worthwhile end. Both will eat anything at any time, unless it is good for them, and they aid and abet each other in socially deplorable ways.

Little children, male or female, adore kittens—never mind that kittens grow into cats who scratch furniture or climb the curtains. Children will rearrange their lives, not to mention their parents' schedules, to suit the habits of a guinea pig, gerbil, or hamster—forget the fact that guinea pigs, gerbils, and hamsters perform no useful task. They are, after all, *pets* —a position of status in a home that protects them from work

30

or responsibility. Or even punishment for misdeeds, which are plentiful.

This writer's family currently has one eleven-year-old dog—of unknown pedigree but possibly from a good neighborhood. We also have two guinea pigs, one of which was purchased at a charity auction, during which no one would bid a single penny against the initial dollar offered by the little girl in the front row, even though they were encouraged—nay begged—by the auctioneer, who was also her father. The other guinea pig is on loan from a friend who has left the state. These animals follow a long line of predecessors, including gerbils, hamsters, several aquaria of fish, and—very briefly—a white mouse.

As many parents have learned, every child who has pets must necessarily have access to adults who can feed and care for the animals. More than once, in moments of desperation, this parent has issued ringing ultimatums: "Either the dog (or guinea pig, mouse, etc.) goes, or I go!" On every occasion the silent weighing of the choice in the minds of the children has caused the ultimatum to be withdrawn.

Please understand. It's nice for children to have pets— until the pets start having children. ("I don't know how it happened, Daddy, I put Harold and Hannah in separate cages every night when I went to bed.") And what adult is so stone-hearted as to object to the warm snuggling of a fat little guinea pig that has been thrust onto his lap by a child? Answer: the one who remembers that the same snuggler once relieved itself all over a pair of freshly pressed slacks!

Even well-behaved pets cause anxiety. Why does a dog delight in sitting in front of a person all evening, staring with pleading, supplicating eyes until the poor human feels like a brute for ignoring it? Why do guinea pigs prefer lettuce (at this point in time ninety cents a head) and squeal for it without ceasing every time the refrigerator opens? Why do children insist their parents love pets as much as they do?

Why, indeed? The answer is—we don't know. We know dogs often love people who are selfish, inconsiderate, and stubborn, but we don't know why. Nor do we know what there is within us which enables fully grown persons to love animals that don't do anything to "deserve" their affection. A guinea pig literally performs no useful function—except to be the object of affection. It is as if they exist to be fed, stroked, fondled, and rubbed, needing no excuse and offering no explanation for affection received.

Perhaps such phenomena show us God's ways at work. Maybe it's one more sign of our need *both* to love and be loved. At times we're too afraid or too insecure to express either need with other humans, so pets allow us to be what God intended us to be—loving, caring, and tender.

If pets remind us that love is its own excuse for being, their existence is justified. It frees us from the notion that we have to justify ourselves by our deeds or our actions. It gives us a glimpse of the grace of God. It can also enable some of us to tolerate, if not celebrate, the birth of more—O Lord, how many more?—guinea pigs.

A Cottage by the Lake

As we grow older, our tastes in vacations change. The desire to see the world—or even America first—is dampened by outrageous gasoline prices and painful memories of traveling long distances with small children in crowded cars. At the same time, spending a vacation at home fails to satisfy the longing for a change of pace and routine, especially when, no matter where we sit, we can always see something that needs to be fixed or cleaned.

Hence, the choice for the middle-aged is to vacation at a nice little cottage by a quiet little lake. This, we reason, will enable us to avoid the dull familiarity of home as well as the masochism of long, car-bound trips with children who begin to ask "How much farther is it, Daddy?" ten minutes after departure. A vacation at the lake spares us much of the pain normally associated with having fun.

It does not remove it entirely, however. One trouble with cottages on a lake is that most of those escaping to them arrive at precisely the same time. Thousands seeking solitude flock to lakes. They come pulling boats with large motors which in turn pull persons on skis who pull muscles while being pulled by the boats. They are greeted by friendly merchants raising rents and food prices, and they experience that special camaraderie of trying, somehow, to dispose of their garbage. Summer cottages become places where parents wait for their teenagers who have driven into town to play miniature golf.

Because many vacationers seek rest in comfortable surroundings, the furniture and conveniences of a cottage are important considerations. Most summer places, however, are furnished in one of two ways. Either they are filled with old overstuffed couches and chairs taken from the attic, or they are occupied with special "leisure furniture" designed in Denmark.

With old stuff you usually get some outstanding fringe benefits. Chances are you will have a sofa long enough to stretch out on—if its musty odor doesn't cause you to wake suddenly from a nap thinking you have been embalmed. No two pieces of furniture and no two dishes match when attics and garage sales have been the source of supply. The decor is inevitably Early Leftover or Late Salvation Army. Yet, lest we forget, in such surroundings we can put our feet up on the couch without guilt feelings and break a dinner plate without tears.

"Leisure furniture" definitely looks nicer, and its designers have shown that "form follows function." Unfortunately, the forms they follow are not always human ones. Metal chairs with criss-crossed leather thongs look super in *House by the Lake* magazine, but while sitting one always appears to be oozing through the holes. Nor is it easy to feel "at home" while sitting in a chair made of aluminum tubing that supports a plastic seat shaped like a bedpan.

The decor and comfort of a cottage by the lake are not small matters. Its interiors take on special meaning when it rains—and it *has* been known to rain during one's vacation period. Veteran vacationers can usually recall a time they spent a week at the lake accompanied by the greatest amount of precipitation since the Johnstown flood.

This ability to recall such memories shows that group experiences of cabin fever can be impressed upon our psyches forever, even if our nervous ticks eventually disappear. When all available books have been read and when one has won ten consecutive games of Scrabble but does not care, the time has arrived for gritting the teeth and repeating three times: "I *am* having fun! I am *having* fun! I am having *fun!*"

An important spiritual insight is hidden somewhere among the musty furniture, the toaster that doesn't work, and the mosquitoes driven inside by the rain. The message is that the *people* in a place are the key to the *joy* of a place. Families that get along well at home will get along well when rain cancels a hike in the woods. Persons who share household tasks back at the ranch will manage with the several inconveniences a cottage provides. If solitude is denied, new acquaintances will supply a happy substitute.

Those able to enjoy a cottage by the lake, leaks and all, are also able to enjoy trips in the car or staying home. The truth is that cottages are only fun when there are people inside. If we can celebrate life with the living, inanimate objects cannot defeat us. For what would it profit us if we had the neatest, fanciest, classiest cottage in the whole world, but no one with whom to share it? That sounds awful, much worse than a broken toaster or a musty couch.

Prayer: "Creator God, prevent our getting too wrapped up in possessions, even a cottage by the lake. Be present in our midst, releasing a spirit of hospitality and cheerfulness, especially when it rains. In the name of him who told us to build houses on rock, not sand. Amen."

III SONGS FOR THE UNSUNG

The church has been seduced by the media. Just as television performers, movie stars, and sports celebrities influence what we eat for breakfast, wear to bed, or use as deodorant, so have the faith and practice of religious life been affected by media visibility.

The personal testimony of a movie star who found God while on location for his most recent picture is reported by Rona Barrett alongside that same star's second wife's present affair. John Jones, the butcher, who finds God in a little Baptist church in Podunk, is considerably less newsworthy.

Church members expend time, energy, and large sums of money to see and hear the Big Stars of Gospel music. They are turned on by large rallies that feature three-hundred voice choirs. By comparison, the little brown church in the wildwood seems very little, very brown, and not at all wild. Its choir consists of nine people, two of whom sing off-key.

While not readily admitting it, our attentions and preoccupations indicate that, in religious as well as in secular life, bigger is better, spectacular is superior, and, while God is no respecter of persons, dramatic religious experiences play better on TV than dull ones.

The following essays—which admittedly will do little to correct the imbalance—are written in praise for the little people, the small tasks, the foot soldiers in God's mighty army. They are written mostly out of experience, some of which was boring but all of which points to the people and events which set the stage for bigger acts in God's drama. The essays are based, also, on observation—taking notice of the contributions of people who are only obvious when they're missing. Newspaper boys and girls are nonentities until they are late with deliveries. Moms are taken for granted until dinner is late. Churches are ignored until they go out of business and decadence prevails in a community.

Hence, we sing songs for the previously unsung. One grudging ballad is for committees, those groups which the church can scarcely live with or do without.

We praise, too, those courageous souls, those Daniels and Danielles, who wrestle young lions in Vacation Church School.

Nor can God's doorkeepers be overlooked, the men and women who think of the church primarily as a building but who, therefore, free others to see it as a Movement.

Parents of small children will join in a hymn of thanksgiving for those special saints who take their turns in the nursery and "suffer little children" as they come.

Several words and delicious memories are offered for potluck suppers, existential proof that local churches care more about food on the table than pie-in-the-sky.

Finally, we say a few kind words for sermons, even bad ones, for we need the one to appreciate the other.

Paul said, "We have this treasure in earthen vessels." Thank God for the treasure, and here are six cheers for the vessels.

On Committees

The church remembers its martyrs and honors its saints. It recalls reformers with pride and extols the virtues of its pioneers. Overlooked in the pages of Christian history, however, has been the committee.

There are several reasons for this oversight, one of which is that the historical review committee had difficulty gathering a quorum and, when they finally got one, couldn't agree. There are other reasons, too, the kind that have given committees a bad name. It has been said, for example, that a committee is a group of the unprepared, appointed by the unwilling, to do the unnecessary. This explains why committees have never received a single line of recognition in the twenty-volume set of *Great Moments in Religious History.*

Indeed, membership on a church committee (often referred to as "standing" rather than "doing") is usually accepted with a degree of enthusiasm associated with washing the dog. The word "committee" is, in fact, a noun signifying "many," but in the minds of most it means "not much."

The writer of Ecclesiastes probably had just returned from a committee meeting when he recorded: "What has been is what will be, and what has been done is what will be done; and there is nothing new under the sun" (1:9). Many good ideas have died of strangulation when referred to a committee, for after all is said and done, more usually has been said than done. Had Moses been a committee, the Israelites might still be in Egypt.

Business executives, who make Big Dollar decisions daily, when on a church committee will become more cautious and indecisive than a kid in a candy store with one nickel. Individuals who are assertive and forthright the rest of the time will table motions, seek more information, and appeal for six weeks of intensive prayer when serving on a committee to buy a new bulletin board. Sometimes the only business that gets done is setting a time for the next meeting, and many church members secretly believe that the best committee consists of three people, two of whom cannot attend.

Even so, churches have found no substitute for committees. Despotism has been tried, but even when it was enlightened it denied people in general the opportunity to share in the work of the church.

Yes, committee work is tedious, redundant, frequently boring, and seldom glamorous. It is like sitting in a soft, overstuffed chair—easy to get into, hard to get out of, and terribly sleep-inducing. Nevertheless, a word of praise must be offered for all those good souls who meet and plan and plan to meet again.

We honor those men and women who go out in the rain, drive across town, and listen to reports. We offer thanks for those who meet in committees to fix roofs, select hymnals, establish budgets, write minutes, and discuss business *ad snoozeum*. Committee work is not the only work of the church nor often the most important business it carries on, but it needs to be done.

The roof, after all, must be fixed. The hymnals wear out. Annual bazaars do not simply happen; they require more planning than the overthrow of a small Latin American government and produce a similar amount of chaos. But let us not forget that the money bazaars raise helps sick children in Africa and starving people in Asia.

If ever a church were to eliminate committees, it would have to appoint a committee to plan their elimination. Who knows? Maybe the reason the kingdom of God has not come in its entirety is because it has been held up in a celestial committee! On the other hand, it might be even farther away without them.

Whatever the case, Christians can only work and hope for its coming. Part of our work, for better or worse, requires participation in committees where rewards are few and progress is slow. We can be sustained, however, by the faith that God's will ultimately prevails; eventually his purposes will be fulfilled. In the meantime we can learn the discipline of patience, and if we learn its lesson well we can taste the sweetness of those welcome words, "The meeting is adjourned."

Prayer for committees: "O Lord, increase our efficiency and spare us unnecessary meetings. If there is a better way, show us, O God. If there isn't, grant us patience. In the name of him who bore a cross. Amen."

On Vacation
Church School

Adult Christians continually fret about bringing up children in the faith. They buy fleets of buses, provide expensive educational facilities, and crank out curriculum materials in four colors, hoping their children will someday resemble Christians.

Thus, worship services feature sermons for children, much to the delight of adults who finally are able to understand something the preacher says. Furthermore, it is not every Sunday they get to see their minister wear a lampshade on his head to illustrate how important it is for Christians to let their lights shine.

Summer brings a special form of this concern into existence, namely, that venerable institution called Vacation Church School. Conscientious parents have learned that with careful planning and theological indifference their children can be kept busy for weeks under the care of Nazarenes, Baptists, Episcopalians, or whoever is geographically convenient.

The intentions of Vacation Church School are noble. The commitment of time, money, and energy is significant. It is important, however, to keep one's hopes in perspective about this enterprise, as well as about all other programs having to do with the nurture of children. Secular society, normal adolescent drives, and original sin work mightily to disrupt the best-laid plans of mice and teachers.

Consider, for example, the literal way children interpret adult teaching:

Teacher: "The children of Israel crossed the Red Sea. They built altars and made sacrifices. Later, they built a big temple."

Child: "Didn't the grown-ups do anything?"

Or, children bring a kind of logic to biblical material that few writers of curricula anticipate:

Teacher: "What can we learn from the story of Jonah and the great fish?"

Child: "People make whales sick?"

Sometimes they *add* information to a traditional story, updating it to fit their own experience:

Teacher: "Johnny, it's very interesting that your drawing shows Joseph, Mary, and the baby Jesus riding in an airplane. But who is the other person with them?"

Child: (patiently) "Aw, that's Pontius the Pilot."

Often they learn lessons other than those their teachers intended. Asked what she had learned from a carefully designed project of making religious stickers for window panes, one girl replied: "I learned that if you get too much water on the stickers, they won't stick." No wonder teachers are tempted to send children home from vacation church school with notes pinned to their shirts saying, "The opinions expressed by this child concerning God, the Bible, morality, things present and things to come, do not necessarily reflect those of the teacher, this church, or the denomination."

Still, given the fact that we're saved by the grace of God and not by our own best efforts, children *may* grow in faith and knowledge, in spite of considerable evidence to the contrary. Many will have the positive experience of watching adult Christians—their teachers—function under tension and pressure, most of which they caused. The fortunate ones will conclude that at least some adults are, in many ways, salvageable.

They will also gain experience in relating to their peers after hearing again and again the importance of "loving others." Little Janie may resist tripping little Susie, even though Susie called her a "turkey." This resistance to doing evil is clear evidence of the power of love and the presence of a very alert teacher. George, age eleven, will learn to overcome his disappointment, nay, humiliation, at having been beaten out by a girl for the role of Goliath in the final-day pageant. Many little ones will go to their homes bearing gifts for their parents, their own enthusiasm transforming a styrofoam and toothpick centerpiece into a work of art.

Maybe, in fact, the honesty, open-mindedness, and enthusiasm children demonstrate are lessons adults can learn from them. Unless we become like children, Jesus said, we can't enter the kingdom. If you're a Vacation Church School teacher, you're necessarily going to have to like children—if not be like them—just to make it to Saturday.

Prayer: "O God, source of courage, we remember that you sustained men and women of old—in fiery furnaces, the face of enemies, and times of pestilence. Stand by us again, O Lord, through Vacation Church School. In the name of him who wouldn't let his disciples send the children away. Amen."

On the Blessed
Doorkeepers

Local churches are resilient. They manage to survive unexpected pastoral changes, ineffective committees, and internal conflicts that make Arabs and Israelis seem good buddies in comparison. From time to time tornadoes or termites destroy church buildings, and congregations sell enough rummage and baked goods to rebuild.

It is less certain, however, that any local church could survive without a janitor. Some churches, in fact, have custodians who rule their buildings as if they were kingdoms, exercising power and authority second in awesomeness only to lifeguards or band directors, and far greater than that of the Joint Chiefs of Staff.

The longer a janitor is around, the more power he collects. He is the only one who knows where the Christmas decorations are kept. He controls the thermostat, and it is usually no coincidence that the heating pipes rattle when the sermon goes on too long. He alone has the fuses needed when the electronic guitars of the Gospel Rock Band throw the entire building into total darkness, and the d-e-l-i-b-e-r-a-t-e way he corrects a problem may very well be his judgment on the music.

Unafraid of man, beast, or the head of the Women's Auxiliary, strong-willed janitors often control activities to fit their own schedules. St. Peter may have the keys to the gates of heaven, but ol' Jerry, the janitor, has the only one to the church basement—and he can make it harder to enter than the Celestial City.

The church building is his domain, and its floors shine because of Jerry's hard work and a congregation so intimidated it fears to walk on them. Cleanliness is still *next* to Godliness, but for Jerry it at least rates equal time.

Not all custodians are so tyrannical, of course. Some seem nearly invisible. They are like gremlins who say little but do much. While they would be offended by the comparison, they are like garbage collectors whose work is never appreciated until it doesn't get done. They become conspicuous only by their absence.

No matter if two feet of snow arrives at five o'clock on a Sunday morning. When worshipers arrive at the regular hour, the walks are clear and the steps are clean and the building is warm. Yet Charlie, the custodian, shows no sign of strain, and one wonders if he has special connections with the Creator.

Neither Charlie nor Jerry gets paid very much, of course, and janitors don't occupy a very high rung on any social ladder. Even so, many church custodians take enormous pride in their work. At their best both Jerry and Charlie demonstrate great love for the church. Jerry has undoubtedly scared many a teenager into cleaning up his mess, which is no small lesson to teach and learn. Charlie frees us from discomfort and inconvenience, and if worshipers are unable to commune with God on Sunday, it won't be because their feet are cold or the hymnals out of place.

The Psalmist may have had them in mind when he wrote, "I would rather be a doorkeeper in the house of my God than dwell in the tents of wickedness" (Ps. 84:10).

Blessed are the doorkeepers, like Jerry and Charlie. May their joys and their salaries increase. Thank God they have chosen to maintain, guard, and protect houses of God rather than tents of wickedness. With them on the church's side, we have one more reason to believe that the gates of hell will not prevail. For who Down There will open them after regular hours or check them for rust? Not Jerry and Charlie. They're elsewhere, making sure the youth group doesn't scuff the golden streets.

Prayer for Custodians: "O God, we know that you do not dwell in a house made with hands. Yet we thank you for those who care for our church buildings. Make us grateful and remind us to wipe our feet before entering. In the name of him who tidied up a temple. Amen."

On Keeping the Nursery

The problem: Your wife wants to hear a particular sermon on a certain Sunday, but she's already promised to supervise the nursery that day.

The solution: You, a veteran parent already on record as favoring sexual equality in child-rearing, volunteer to take her place. Assisting you will be your thirteen-year-old son and your nine-year-old daughter, whose commitment to Christian service is transcended only by the belief that helping in the nursery beats sitting through church.

Five minutes before the worship service begins, nine children under six years of age arrive. Their parents, upon discovering that their progeny are to be left for an hour in your care, express surprise and anxiety. "Are *you* keeping the nursery today?" The question is asked in a tone of voice normally used in addressing lepers. Relief comes when you explain that you have a nine-year-old and a thirteen-year-old helping.

You are barraged with instructions. "The diapers for Joanie are in this bag, and tissues—you know, in case you need them." (Diapers!? Tissues!?)

"Billy's teething, so he may cry a little at first, but he'll quiet right down if you rock him for awhile." (Does she mean I am to hit him with a rock?)

"Stevie is a little shy at first, but he'll be fine after I leave."

(Stevie has wrapped both legs and arms around his mother's waist and is screaming and kicking.)

Suddenly you are the only adult in a room full of children. The nursery is well equipped with dozens of toys, a miniature slide, and a simple phonograph for playing tunes to take naps by. Why, then, do three of the children insist on riding the same rocking horse at once?

You attempt to negotiate a settlement. It is not easily transacted, however, as calm discussion is deterred by one child throwing a leg over the wooden animal and another responding by biting him on the ankle.

"Michael, we don't bite people on the ankle just because they went out of turn. Now both you and Phillip will have to wait until Sarah has her turn." Sarah, however, has managed to climb the slide to its four-foot height. You turn just in time to see her shoot down head-first backwards, landing with sufficient impact to produce a scream last heard when Tarzan called elephants.

You rush to comfort Sarah, leaving the rocking horse negotiations to your son. You are gratified to learn she will live to call elephants another day, and her parents will not be filing suit against you after all.

The moment for rejoicing passes quickly, however. Why do the three infants need diaper changes one after the other at five-minute intervals? Changing diapers was never as much fun as a picnic, but having the diaperee's sister dance about the table chanting "Nora did a poo-poo" adds little to the experience. It does, however, call attention to the event, and you are suddenly aware that all eyes are riveted upon you. They have discovered a spectator sport more fascinating than riding a rickety rocking horse or sliding head-first backward.

You seize the moment. A flick of the wrist sends Johnson's powder to its intended and freshly cleaned target. With one hand you pin a diaper, smiling broadly to cover the pain of having stuck the pin into your thumb. The entire group accompanies you as you rinse the dirty diaper in the toilet with one hand while balancing Nora on your hip with the other. Respect—nay, awe—glistens in their eyes.

Your helper-daughter suggests the distribution of a graham cracker snack. It is an idea whose time has come, since Joanie has started to chew on a purple crayon. Meanwhile, back in the playpen, Elizabeth has finished her bottle and is letting all know it is time for relief—spelled b-u-r-p.

For you, relief is spelled f-i-n-a-l h-y-m-n, and the sound of the organ playing is more welcome than the bugle of the cavalry coming to the rescue. The faces of the children glow with happiness, a joy second only to that felt by the keepers of the nursery. Two children remove their thumbs from their mouths long enough to wave good-bye, and Stevie wraps both arms and legs around your waist and yells that he doesn't want to leave.

Keeping the nursery fulfills Scripture, particularly the passage where it says, "Suffer the little children to come." "Suffer" in the King James Version didn't mean what it does today, but it should. The word reminds the keeper that he's middle-aged, and that for every good thing under the sun there is a season. The natural order clearly indicates that *young* adults were intended to be parents of little children.

Yes, we know that Abraham and Sarah in the Old Testament got a late start, and every now and then we hear of couples in their fifties raising babies. Most of us, however, rejoice in the selected memories of our children when they were small. An occasional tour of duty in the nursery reminds us why we stopped having children when we did. Three diaper changes in twelve minutes are sufficient to meet all nostalgic needs to jump backward in time.

Blessed are the persons who supervise the nursery week after week. May they have joy and peace all the days of their lives—and plenty of diapers near at hand.

On Church Suppers

The church supper is an excellent argument for active participation in a local congregation. This statement may sound surprising, since critics of the local church often associate church suppers with bingo and rummage sales as examples of nominal Christianity. The late Harry Golden was clear in his criticism of the church supper phenomenon: "The first part of a church they build nowadays is the kitchen. Five hundred years from now, people will dig up these churches, find the steam tables, and wonder what kind of sacrifices we performed."

Why, then, do we here honor church suppers? We do so for many reasons, both major and minor. For one thing church suppers provide many families with an alternative to three other eating options: (1) eating at home, (2) eating in a restaurant, or (3) eating at a formal dinner party.

Eating at home bears the burden of excessive familiarity. The dishes are the same, the décor is the same, and whoever sets the table invariably forgets the napkins. The conversation is often a rehash of what's gone before, and—given the economic necessity of consuming leftovers—so, frequently, is the meal. Dinnertime is likely to be structured around a TV schedule, and *somebody* eventually has to do the dishes.

Eating in restaurants where we sit down and order from a menu is expensive. It solves the napkin problem, but these days a diner will have to find a pearl in the oyster soup to break even. Nevertheless, hope springs eternal in the human heart—which explains why new restaurants are crowded. The food is often good and usually arrives the same day the order is taken, but—like death and taxes—the check inevitably arrives as well.

Formal dinner parties avoid the familiar surroundings of home and are cheaper than eating in a restaurant, unless you're the host. The word *formal*, however, conveys a certain amount of anxiety, as those who attend sometimes experience tension. Which fork do I use? What if I spill the soup on their oriental rug? If corn-on-the-cob is served, guests will necessarily have to make a split-second decision—should we be fastidious or enjoy it? As a matter of fact, basic food such as corn-on-the-cob is seldom served. What *is* served is creamed cheese on celery, a delicacy just right for formal dinners, even though it sounds as if we are stepping on a basket when we eat it.

Church suppers, however, have the benefits of the above without their liabilities. The surroundings are different from home, the food is inexpensive, and the mood is casual. At that special kind of church supper—the "pitch-in" (also called "carry-in" or "covered dish")—two miracles regularly occur: (1) There is always enough to eat, even though fourteen visitors show up unexpectedly, and (2) there is always a balance of meat, vegetables, salad, and dessert, in spite of the fact no one plans it that way.

The latter miracle is not totally appreciated by small children in attendance. Their idea of a balanced meal is a plate loaded with two chocolate cupcakes, banana and strawberry jello (with whipped cream), a piece of fudge cake, and a pickle. Veterans of the carry-in supper, however, come looking for specialties of the congregation. Aunt Minerva always brings her Dutch apple strudel, a dish so delicious it previews the great Church Supper we will one day eat in the sky. Mrs. Jones dependably presents her offering of chicken potpie, which is based on a secret recipe and cooked at night with shades drawn and doors locked. Mrs. Goodbody competes for attention with sourdough bread, and all who eat it are twice-blessed. Unlike the food in the homemaker magazines, at church suppers it's the taste—not the photography—that's superb.

The real benefit of a church supper, however, is the quality of its fellowship. Such occasions are usually intergenerational, a fancy name for little kids eating with people old enough to be their grandparents. Often, too, they manifest the extended family, another popular phrase describing single people mingling with married people, couples without children sharing their napkins with somebody else's chocolate-smeared toddler, and teenagers sitting with their parents. The church supper, in fact, provides authentic communion among persons who otherwise would be segregated from one another. And, if nothing else, they help single people rejoice in their singleness and reduce the nostalgia of grandparents for their grandchildren.

Even the cleaning up is an act of fellowship. The children get to wad up the paper table cloth and stuff it into the trash. Boys-becoming-men and men-acting-like-boys fold the tables and put them away. Men who never do a dish at home immerse their arms in a sinkful at church, and many a serving dish—presumably lost forever—is rediscovered, a prodigal from a previous dinner come home.

Church suppers, like any other human event, can be exclusive and boring. Sometimes they are used as bribes, arranged to tempt people to attend a business meeting or to hear a dull speaker. Occasionally they are only fund-raising affairs to which people come and buy the food they've spent half the day preparing.

Nevertheless, the theology of Christians is often expressed in the quality of their church suppers. Just as the way families think, talk, and behave in the unguarded informality of the home is a clue to their real values, so is the way Christians act at their "family" suppers a clue to their sense of brother/ sisterhood. Those fourteen outsiders who drop in unexpectedly on our church supper will likely form judgments about our fellowship more on the basis of what they see, hear, and taste than what we *say* about ourselves.

Certainly the standard for Christian fellowship is high, much higher than any church supper could fully reveal. Yet it was no coincidence that the book of Acts records the vitality of the early church by saying the Christians "shared their meals with unaffected joy, as they praised God and enjoyed the favour of the whole people" (Acts 2:46, NEB). Breaking bread together breaks barriers as well.

A friendly, informal, inclusive church supper can demonstrate real caring and sharing. Wouldn't it be grand, in fact, if those who attended our church suppers came away thinking, "Those Christians—how they enjoy one another!"

P.S. As a sideline, some of them make excellent chicken potpie.

On Sermons

Five million sermons a year are preached in the United States. The number remembered is undoubtedly smaller, but the fact remains that preaching is still a central event in the life of the church.

For many, it is safe to say, all else that occurs in a Sunday service is preliminary or anticlimactic. The hymns and responsive readings are only warm-ups for the "main event," and the success or failure of the worship service is determined by how good or how bad the sermon is. John Calvin, no less, was vehement against those who would minimize preaching to magnify the Lord's Supper: "Without the word, the sacrament is but a dumb show; the word must go before." John Churchgoer, local Protestant, essentially is agreeing when he remarks to the preacher, "I want to get over and hear you some Sunday."

Preaching, however, is not held in high regard by all who listened to last year's five million sermons. Indeed, some objections to preaching are severe. People say it is not suited to "our time." The very words "preach" and "preachy" have negative connotations, as in "Don't preach to me," or "I need help, not a sermon." One midwestern judge sentenced a man to a year's attendance at the church of his choice with the additional requirement of taking notes each Sunday on the sermon. Was the intent rehabilitation or punishment?

Jokes about dull sermons are plentiful and familiar:

"The difference between a good sermon and a bad one is a nap."

"The eternal gospel does not require an everlasting sermon."

"If all the people who sleep in church were placed end to end, they would be more comfortable."

If, in fact, all the jokes about dull sermons were placed end to end, they would more than fill a pew.

The jokes, unfortunately, are grounded in reality. There are many sermons which are dull or trivial or irrelevant. Some manage to be all three! In fact, one of the strongest proofs of the Gospel is the preaching it has survived. Let's face it—many sermons are finished long before the preacher quits talking.

Sermons are often too long. Most congregations would agree with Mark Twain: "Few sinners are saved after the first twenty minutes of a sermon." Even brief sermons can be boring and trivial, and many short ones, delivered straight from the shoulder, would have been better if the preacher's words had started a little higher up. Way down deep, many sermons are shallow.

What's the church to do? Protestantism has never found a substitute for preaching, and the use of films, tapes, modern dance, choral readings, or pantomime gets less positive response than a good sermon. If no substitute is a consistent improvement, can we do better with what we have?

Two circumstances are needed if a high view of the sermon is to be justified and a low opinion overcome. Both better preaching and better listening need to occur. The one is dependent upon the other. Many a churchgoer's idea of a good sermon is one that goes over his head and hits someone else. In other words a lack of *interest* in preaching, by both preachers and listeners, is directly related to their commitment to the Christian faith. Merely going to church doesn't make one a Christian any more than sleeping in a garage makes you a car.

A people hungry for the Word of God and its application to life will inspire mediocre preaching to be better. Good preaching will evoke a response—sometimes appreciation, often commitment, and occasionally disagreement. High expectations for sermons will remind ministers that sloppy preparation will not be tolerated, and good preaching will be connected to real life. Good sermons, in effect, will be multiplied—in the same proportion as there are people in the congregation.

When sermons come alive, at least two good results will occur. The Gospel will be preached—no mean achievement. And television will then assume its deserved place as the great sleep-inducer of our time.

Prayer for Sermons: "O Lord, be present in the churches, so that preaching and listening to sermons will begin and end at the same time. In the name of him who came preaching. Amen."

IV VIRTUE RECONSIDERED

A *Boy Scout, as everyone knows, is trustworthy, loyal, helpful,* friendly, courteous, kind, obedient, cheerful, thrifty, brave, clean, and reverent. So are many Christians. So, too, are a surprising number of pagans, though they have some trouble with the last virtue in the list. Reverence, therefore, is interpreted by pagans as a form of courtesy—taking one's hat off at gravesides and addressing clergy as "reverend." For the most part, genial pagans behave a lot like genial Christians.

The apostle Paul, however, was picky about the *source* of virtues. He did not have a high opinion of law or lists as the motivation for virtue, whether it be Jewish or Scout. In Galatians 5:22–25 he spoke directly to the point: "The harvest of the Spirit is love, joy, peace, patience, kindness, goodness, fidelity, gentleness, and self-control. There is no law dealing with such things as these. . . . If the Spirit is the source of our life, let the Spirit also direct our course" (NEB).

In other words virtue flows out of a Christian's relationship to God: we love because he first loved us. Good behavior is dynamic, not static. Doing the right thing comes from trying each day in each new situation to be God's person. Much of the time, of course, how we are supposed to behave is predictable. So we make lists of virtues and forget that the virtues are "the *harvest* of the Spirit."

Yes, we're called to be brave, but what courage means varies from instance to instance. Clearly, it can be interpreted in many more ways than offered in the stereotypes of cowboys and truck drivers.

The energy crisis is forcing all of us Scouts to become thrifty. When we continually examine and reexamine our values in the light of Christ, frugality is inspired long before the wells run dry. It is practiced out of obedience.

Self-control is not itself the Good News, for as anyone knows who's practiced it to some degree, it often hurts. It also tempts us to self-righteousness when we succeed. It feels different, however, when we experience God's Spirit in the practice of discipline.

Patience, which made Paul's list, is possible when we are convinced the end for which we're waiting is worthwhile. We will wait for our doctor to see us because our physical health is at stake. The question is: Are we able to "wait upon the Lord?"

Contentment, kindred spirit to patience, comes with the learning of the seasons. The passing of time—summer, winter, spring, and fall—is necessary before we can know happiness transcends the weather.

Humility, by its own name, didn't make either list. Yet it may be the best illustration of Paul's point: we *find* ourselves as we *lose* ourselves.

Loyal, courteous, brave, patient, and gentle readers, the following essays deal with nothing new. They serve only to remind us that God in Christ did more than provide us with a list of virtues which merely reveal our failures. God gave us his Spirit which is both the source and the direction for our lives.

Actually, that's a relief! When all the virtues are written out and put on lists, the Christian life is too formidable to attempt. The laws of the Pharisees and the laws of the Scouts, by themselves, are both overwhelming. "Thou shalt not" for the struggler is as tough to manage as "thou shall knot" is for the Scout. Doing the right thing under any system is difficult, but doing the right things for the right reasons makes it worthwhile.

Cowboys and
Truck Drivers

In the good old days we indulged our fantasies about rugged individualism by attending cowboy movies at the local theater. The plot of the movie was always the same:

> The
> Two-fisted,
> Tight-jawed,
> Fleet-footed,
> Slim-hipped,
> Ox-strong
> Hero
> Crossed the screen,
> Curled his lip,
> Maimed the Villain,
> Kissed the Heroine,
> And it was
> THE END.

In a typical Western movie the hero was strong and silent, not quite as pretty as the heroine and only slightly smarter than his horse. He was a Real Man, however, and he personified the days when men were men and women liked it. We would watch him on the silver screen and, in the darkness, project our own desires to be free, strong, tough, modest, and brave.

Today, cowboy movies are more complicated. The heroes

aren't much different from the villains and, in keeping with the cynicism of our times, the good guys don't always win. Psychological explanations are suggested by the script for the behavior of all the characters except the horses who, as a result, frequently steal the show.

For better or worse, however, a substitute for the cowboy has emerged from out of the West (Hollywood), this time driving a truck. No longer do we hear the "thundering hoofbeats of the great horse, Silver!" Now we are treated to the raucous blare of the great air horns, and the call of the frontier is by Citizens Band radio.

Similarities between cowboys and truck drivers are more striking than differences. Both sit tall in the saddle, eight feet above contradiction. The truck driver drives a mechanical beast, to be sure, but it is still horsepower on which he depends for strength and vitality.

Cowboys on the trail slept on the ground and ate bad food cooked over an open fire. Truck drivers sleep in their cabs and survive on greasy-spoon Disco Burgers—so called because they hop up and down in the stomach the whole night long.

The cowboy and his horse were inseparable. Whatever the odds, Ol' Paint, Trigger, or Silver would leap gullies, swim rivers, or attack coyotes for their masters. In trucker movies, drivers crash through roadblocks, flatten automobiles, and smash buildings—and the "Blue Goose" or "Diesel Darling" responds faithfully with all its cylinders.

Of course, cowboy nicknames sounded more virile and ominous than their trucker counterparts. "Black Bart" or "The Lone Ranger," when growled on the silver screen, carried a quality of he-man-ness that the words, "This is the Rubber Duck, c'mon," cannot match. Yet, as attenders of trucker movies know, the plot is an updated version of the basic Western:

The
Two-fisted,
Unshaven,
Broad-beamed,
Quick-shifting,
Trucker
Puts the hammer down,
Talks on the CB,
Smashes the roadblock,
Delivers the goods,
And it is
THE END.

Perhaps every age needs its romantic heroes and heroines. For those whose lives seem routine, even dull, who feel trapped by work and badgered by the boss, the "maverick," be he cowboy or trucker, provides a welcome relief. In a world in which the good guys lose on the news programs, it may be necessary to fix it so they win in the feature movie.

No harm is done if we remind ourselves that reality and fantasy are not the same. Tough, independent good guys (and women) are needed in the world, but their lives will seldom be as glamorous or their circumstances as simplistic as those depicted in the trucker movies.

The Christian hero or heroine, moreover, will always be fundamentally different from either the cowboy or the truck driver. He or she will never be completely free and independent. The Christian will always be seeking and attempting to do the will of God, not merely his own. Doing God's will demands more courage than have the Lone Ranger and Mack the Trucker combined. The life of faith is to trust, try, fail, try again, experience forgiveness, and trust some more.

Being strong, independent, and Christian is no job for a Rubber Duck.

Hot Weather Lessons

By the time August arrives, summer has lost its prestige. We've watched enough television reruns to discover that the shows we missed last winter weren't worth seeing in the first place. Our children have spent most of their waking hours slamming doors they left open last winter, and the importance of the school system to the education of the young and the sanity of adults is painfully obvious.

It isn't the heat, exactly, that bothers us. It's the people who keep reminding us of the humidity. Summer brings with it warmer air pollution, so we turn up the air conditioner to make our homes as cool as they were last fall when we gathered around a fire. Indeed, extensive air conditioning has theological implications: hell carries no terrors when our buildings, our cars, and our homes deny its reality.

August, in other words, is the time we decide we like winter better than summer and autumn best of all. Or maybe spring, but definitely not summer. Ironically, we look toward summer all winter, then gripe our way through it, and are sorry when it passes.

God, in fact, may look down upon us and wonder: "Are those creatures *ever* satisfied?" A good question, the kind we might expect from the Creator. Summer becomes the time when it is too hot to do the work it was too cold to do last winter. We go on vacations and come home needing a vacation. Those very things we couldn't wait to do become boring, and poor old August gets blamed for "dog days"—hot, sticky, and depressing.

Yet those who are able to enjoy August have the secret of contentment: *when you haven't what you like, like what you have.* To experience peace of mind, in other words, we simply have to cooperate with the inevitable.

The secret of enjoying "dog days" is a clue to all happiness—namely, to accept the impossible, do without the indispensable, and bear the intolerable. Consider, for example, the way sentences of discontent usually begin:

"It's too hot to . . ."
"I can't wait until . . ."
"If it doesn't rain by tonight, I'm going to . . ."
"I can't bear the thought of . . ."
"If those kids ask once more to . . ."
"I think I'll scream if . . ."

Such sentences reveal our contentment quotient. They illustrate the importance of cooperating with the inevitable. If it really is "too hot to . . . ," then don't. If we *can't* wait until Thursday, we're in bad trouble, because Thursday hurries for no one. If rainfall is a matter of importance, we can either water the grass or watch it turn brown. Few other options are open to us, and screaming will not intimidate the Creator.

The fact is, we *can* bear the thought of a large variety of disappointments and misfortunes. We *already* thought of them when we said we couldn't bear the thought—and the sky didn't fall. And whatever our children ask to do one more time, the probability is that they will ask to do one more time after that. And again and again.

Thus, the familiar prayer of Alcoholics Anonymous is just right for summer: "God grant us the serenity to accept those things that can't be changed, the courage to change those things that ought to be changed, and the wisdom to know the difference."

We can be still more specific: "God grant us enough energy to work in the heat if we must, the memories of cooler climates to sustain us if we live where it's sultry, and the common sense to know that a cantankerous spirit raises the body temperature. Amen."

"Thanks, God—
We Needed That"

The energy crisis is forcing us to change our transportation habits.
This is no mean task, for Americans have been in love with
their automobiles for half a century and using them less is like
rejecting an old friend. One man said, when asked why he
kept his old gas guzzler, "Because it needs me!"

Nevertheless, many of us are deciding that we don't need
cars as much as we thought. This writer's family has
discovered that having an old, dilapidated automobile is an
effective way to ration gasoline. Some of the time—nay,
much of the time—it won't start at all, so we are forced to
walk, ride a bus, or stay at home. When it does manage to
start, we hesitate to travel very far, because it sometimes fails
to finish what it begins. Indeed, a mechanic once suggested
that, were our car a horse, it would have been shot by now.
The young adults in our family, furthermore, do not like to
drive it because it is a source of social embarrassment and so
old-looking the license bureau wanted to issue it both upper
and lower plates.

Old cars, moreover, usually do not get good gas mileage,
and the cost of gasoline is producing more pedestrians each
day. Being "odd" is no longer a derisive term in some states,
except on "even" days. Couples contemplating marriage may
one day be regarded as compatible if their temperaments
agree and their license plates don't.

So we turn to trains and buses and discover that these two
forms of getting from here to there are not always perfect.

Riding a bus is better than riding an oxcart, but new riders soon discover that time, tide, and bus drivers wait for no one. The bus, it seems, is a vehicle that runs twice as fast when you are after it as when you are on it. The rides feature lots of stops and starts, too, and most of the shock absorbers are the passengers.

Trains, particularly subway trains, do not always make getting there half the fun. In fact, one of the reasons many resist doing the sane and patriotic thing of using mass transportation is that the mass is such a mess. Where else can one be squeezed, pushed, hauled, jostled, jerked, buffeted, cursed, crunched, insulted, smashed, tangled, and elbowed in the groin within a thirty-minute period? Only in a big city subway during rush hour!

True, crowded trains sometimes increase our faith and nurture our commitment. We understand more clearly the nature of original sin after being poked in the ribs by an eighty-year-old woman than we did after studying Genesis. And, as perspiring humanity gradually fills the car well past its legal capacity, we spontaneously pray words of gratitude for Dentyne, Listerine, Ban, and all other products that take the worry out of being close.

The energy crisis is real, and neither the problem nor the answer is easy. A key aspect of the Christian message is not the *absence* of problems in the life of the believer, but the sustaining presence of God in the midst of them. In the energy crisis, this faith statement has some clear implications. It is a direct rebuttal to those motorists who insist that if God had intended us to walk, we would not have been born with cars. We are called to discover—if we can—virtue in the midst of adversity.

Long lines at the gasoline stations have produced resentment, anger, even violence. They have also evoked courtesy, kindness, and good humor. Those forced to walk have sometimes discovered joy in walking. Trains and buses generate better service as they are used more, and the air we breathe becomes cleaner when there is less exhaust fouling it. Car pools introduce us to new friends—or teach us tolerance.

The people of Israel became more faithful in tough times, not because faith came naturally for them, but because they rediscovered their dependence upon God and on one another. So can we. Thoreau once said: "Traveling is good which reveals the value of home and enables us to enjoy it better." Exercising, sharing resources, living simply, and practicing courtesy are right, whether or not there is an energy crisis.

Thus, we pray: "Thanks, God. We needed that. Amen."

The "Good-Health" Gospel

What is more self-righteous than a Pharisee, quicker with a testimony than a reformed drunk, and more missionary-minded than the Apostle Paul? You're wrong if you guessed either a friendly neighborhood Mormon or a compulsive Jehovah's Witness. The right answer is . . . a jogger on a diet. Or, if you prefer, a dieter who jogs.

Church members are not usually aggressively evangelistic about their faith. Their evangelism is tentative: "I don't suppose you'd ever want, maybe, to consider, if it's not inconvenient, visiting our church?" That's much different from your born-again jogger who has discovered Good Health. Those folks spread their news to all who will listen and to many who aren't interested.

They talk—more accurately, they proclaim, lecture, expound, preach, and promote—while their audience listens and feels guilty or resentful or both. Their advice is often resented because it's hard to accept the truth; as one overweight nonjogger put it: "Don't you hate it when they're right?"

Alas! Right food and right exercise are good for us. The human body is the baggage we carry on the trip of life, and the more excess luggage we haul around, the shorter the trip. Muscles may come and go, but flab endures. Many Americans are as sound as a dollar—which means they're in a lot of physical trouble.

Unfortunately, the best way to keep healthy is to eat what

we don't want, drink what we do not like, and do what we'd rather not. Given the pain which accompanies early attempts at jogging, beginners are convinced that daily exercise merely enables us to die healthier. Craving the good, rich food that is abruptly denied, a dieter may conclude that losing weight does not actually prolong life—it only seems that way.

Thus, dieting joggers who proclaim the Way to Good Health with evangelical zeal often experience resistance from the unconverted. When confronted with the merits of the "Rockefeller Diet," the uninitiated wonder, "Do you have to be rich to follow it?" Or they respond to the Word about the Mayo diet or the Scarsdale diet or some other twenty-one-day regimen (that always features cottage cheese and thin slices of all-bran sandpaper) with the same enthusiasm Socrates had for hemlock.

However, it's not just theory, but practice, that intimidates or repels nondieting nonjoggers. When a poor soul (translation: overweight and out of breath individual) learns that health addicts really *do* live on two glasses of skim milk, eight prunes, and four lamb kidneys a day, he or she may quickly decide to stay fat and learn how to be jolly. Experienced joggers think nothing of running five miles a day, and rain, sleet, snow, or dark of night will not stay them from their appointed rounds. Nonjoggers don't think much of running five miles, either, and they are easily stayed, whatever the weather.

The analogy between the jogging dieter and the on-fire Christian is apt. The zealous Christian is like the passionate devotee of Good Health in several ways. Both have experienced insights that have changed their lives. Both demonstrate lifestyles that require discipline and commitment. Both have a sense of urgency about sharing the Good News with others. Both practice their faith every day of the week and not just on Sunday.

Unfortunately, both can be obnoxious and self-righteous in the process. This happens when those who have found "It" neglect to remember the pain and agony that accompanied the discovery. The Good News is not that the Christian life is a destination where all is well. It is not a magical transformation that makes the struggle unnecessary or protects the believer from pain.

The Good News is that God does not withhold his presence *until* we shape up. Christ does not deny his support until we've lost twenty pounds and can run five miles without stomach cramps. Christ is with us from the beginning—while we're still spiritually or physically fat, short of breath, and wondering if we can live on prune juice and yogurt. That's really good news, for that's when we need him most.

The Patience
of Patients

The practice of medicine has changed dramatically in recent years.
Medicare and health insurance have enabled us to have
diseases otherwise beyond our means, and medical technique
has advanced so far that it is next to impossible for a doctor
not to find something wrong with us.

Even so, certain medical customs remain unchanged,
particularly in the long, long periods of time spent in that
best-named of all places—the waiting room. Modern doctors
have trained their patients to become sick only during office
hours, and their outer offices are now filled for longer periods
with more people than at any time since the discovery of
gallstones.

Some patients don't mind waiting. A few do so enthusi-
astically. Usually these are hypochondriacs whose ailments
are eagerly shared with all who care to listen and some who
do so only because there was only one available chair when
they arrived.

The aches and pains of the hypochondriac not only are
chronic; they are chronicles. Their conversations sometimes
sound like a medical version of "Can You Top This?"
Abdominal pains outrank sore throats, sore throats have
priority over queasiness, and queasiness is one notch above
backaches. Hemorrhoids are mentioned quickly, of course,
and quietly, as if one were discussing a bribe. For a
hypochondriac, however, nothing spoils a visit to a doctor
faster than someone infringing upon his symptoms.

Really sick people also make waiting room waiting less fun than major surgery: "All things come to him who waits," saith a wise person. However, as one sitteth outside his doctor's door, listening to sniffles, exposed to infections and rashes, and targeted by homeless viruses, one may conclude that among those things that cometh will be an incurable disease.

Should the waiting occur in a pediatric clinic, furthermore, the possibilities for sharing each other's diseases are multiplied. Parents bring small children for shots who, in turn, dash from sick youngster to healthy sibling to community drinking fountain, sowing germs like Johnny Appleseed. Pediatric clinics, therefore, generate their own business, even though families of four or more children often develop immunities because of extensive exposure to every known virus or allergy. Parents of several children also learn medical jargon, particularly the difference between a virus and an allergy. A virus is what a sickness is called when the doctor doesn't know what it is, and "allergy" describes a disease a doctor can identify but can't cure.

Appointments with doctors sometimes occur when scheduled, but veteran patients soon learn never to leave a roast in the oven. And so innocent waiters—those who have come for required physical exams, or to get a doctor's signature on a health form, or (most pathetic of all) the man who got sick on his day off—learn patience, which is a form of despair disguised as a virtue.

To pass time, people in waiting rooms read magazines. Magazines in doctors' offices fall into two categories: (1) Old copies of Today's Health with articles such as "New Techniques in Urinalysis" to fascinate us; and (2) religious tracts entitled "Where Will You Spend Eternity?" left by local Jehovah's Witnesses. As her waiting enters the second hour, a patient may conclude she has found the place and has started spending it.

Our willingness to wait for doctors is instructive. Since health is important, waiting is treated as a necessity, not an imposition. We'll put up with the inconveniences, noise, trials, tribulations, and pestilence—when we're convinced it's worth the wait.

To find spiritual health we may also have to wait upon the Lord. Isaiah stated it clearly: "They who wait for the Lord shall renew their strength, . . . they shall run and not be weary, they shall walk and not faint" (Isa. 40:31).

That is a comforting promise, worth waiting for, especially since the Lord makes house calls, even at night.

Prayer for Patience: "O God, help us to be patient and wait upon you. Thank you for doctors who help us experience your healing, even if they're behind schedule. In the name of the Great Physician. Amen."

Let It Shine Anyhow!

It had been a good year. The school had not only finished in the black; it had also achieved a modest balance from which payment toward past indebtedness could be made. Enrollment in the student body was the largest in the history of the school, and the overall quality of the students was excellent.

When the dean completed his report, a happy faculty broke into applause for itself. Success had not just happened. It was the result of hard work and steady commitment by everybody involved.

The dean had been gone from home so often looking for money that his two-year-old daughter refused to get into the car with him when he returned—her mother had told her never to accept rides with strangers.

The business manager had taped light switches to the "off" position, recycled tea bags, and taken free-will offerings at coffee breaks to stay under budget.

The director of development had visited so many elderly ladies with property to bequeath that his wife had offered to donate her jewelry to the school to catch his attention.

The faculty had done promotional work at so many small churches never before visited that two congregations were discovered which had been assumed disbanded in 1898.

We jest, of course. The point is, nonetheless, that we were pleased with our accomplishments. We deserved our applause.

But then . . . just when the warm glow of satisfaction was

oozing through our bodies, the theologian stood and got our attention. He said we really should praise God for his blessings to us, and he asked us to sing the Doxology with him. Heck! That's the problem in carrying the label, "Christian." We never really get to take the credit. Somebody *always* calls us to "praise God *from whom* all blessings flow."

The New Testament does it, too, just in case nobody remembers. In Matthew 5:16 a reminder sneaks up on us: "Let your light so shine before men, that they may see your good works [a fine idea!] and give glory to your Father who is in heaven [Wouldn't you know!]."

Our inner response, however, may not be so generous. An oft-quoted story accurately represents our feelings: A neighbor comments to a man who had a beautiful garden, laden with vegetables and rich in produce, "You and God surely did a good job on that garden." To this the gardener replies, "Yes, but you should have seen it when God had it on his own."

That's the way we feel, but it doesn't seem appropriate for Christians to take too much credit, even though they've worked harder than beavers making toothpicks. Consequently, we use language with double meanings. This enables us to take credit for our work while seemingly attributing results to the Lord. Consider the following examples:

—"The Lord has richly blessed us." (Translation: "And a sixty-hour work week didn't hurt either.")

—"The Lord works in mysterious ways his wonders to perform." (Translation: "Four committees, two professional consultants, sixteen volunteers, and a media expert used everything but whips and chains to raise the money.")

—"Pastor Goodheart is accepting a call to greater fields of service." (Translation: "Goodheart played ball with the parish relations committee and let everyone in the denomination know he was looking.")

We try to have it both ways. We try to attribute results to Providence while clinging to credit for ourselves. It is the perennial problem of works versus grace. Humility is the trickiest virtue to experience because, like grasping the soap in the shower, when we think we've got it, it slips away. It's hard to talk about it without denying it, e.g. "It's only through the grace of God that I've achieved humility"!

A pagan (nonreligious) perspective has no such dilemma. Those who do not start from the premise that all blessings flow from a gracious God are spared the problem of giving or receiving credit. They can applaud themselves and let others applaud them and be done with it. They don't have to add that second phrase, "and give glory to God in heaven." This may explain, in fact, why there are so many pagans.

The dilemma is not going to disappear. About the time we get the reputation as a spiritual person, we stumble over that verse about praying in our closets. Shortly after we get excited by the idea that "to be Christian is to be *fully human,*" we'll read these words by John Calvin: "We are not our own; therefore neither our reason nor our will should dominate our deliberations and actions. We are not our own; therefore let us not presuppose it as our end to seek what may be expedient for us according to the flesh. . . . On the contrary, we are God's; therefore let his wisdom and will preside in all our actions. We are God's; towards him, therefore, as our only legitimate end, let every part of our lives be directed."

Doggone it, what's a normal, fully human, prideful Christian to do? The answer is just what the Bible says—Let our lights shine! So that the glory of God may be proclaimed. We can run the risk of hypocrisy. We are saved by God's grace whether or not we take the credit.

You think the garden was a mess when God had it on his

own? Have you noticed what humans are doing to the world on their own?

You think that because you organized four committees and recruited sixteen volunteers the project was a success? On the contrary, success that comes out of committees and volunteers is clear evidence of God's miraculous power.

The paradox is that we find ourselves as we lose ourselves. In doing the will of God we discover satisfaction and peace. Occasionally, we also achieve worthwhile goals. Whether we take the credit or give the credit, God's ultimate will is going to be done. Calvin was right. We are not our own. We are God's. Therefore, let our—I mean his—light . . . I mean both his and ours . . . aw, heck, let it shine and leave the bookkeeping to God.

V MOMENTS OF TRUTH

Authentic religious experience is unpredictable. We go to church to worship God, and we may leave with irritation, resentment about the sermon, or the feeling that those who stayed in bed were right after all. Moments that are supposed to be sacramental—when your daughter says her wedding vows or your son joins the church—fall flat due to circumstances beyond your control. Uncle Charles pops a flash bulb at precisely the wrong time, or you get the vague feeling that joining the church is less important to your son than winning the door prize at the sophomore carnival.

Churches do what they can. They try to establish moods of worship and develop rituals designed to encourage worshipers to feel comfortable and open. We send our children to summer camp and hope that the candlelight service by the lake when everybody sings "Kumbaya" will enable them to feel the Spirit. Many Christians practice daily disciplines of meditation, Bible study, and prayer, knowing that preparation for God's presence is essential, but also knowing that many dry and sterile times will be experienced.

Sometimes we do, in fact, experience God's presence at times we've expected to do so. It's safe to say that many Christians *have* experienced it in church. Yet we all know that such experiences cannot be predicted and certainly not controlled by our best-laid plans. Few churches are nervy enough to announce, "Come to our church and we will guarantee a deeply moving religious experience."

It is also true that we experience many unexpected, unplanned, unpredicted moments of grace. They may be "mountaintops"—Paul on the road to Damascus or Charles Colson on the road to prison—or they may be "molehills"—a fresh insight that inches us deeper into our relationship with Christ. Looking back, we sometimes discover the molehills were the foothills leading to the mountaintops.

Authentic Christian experience is connected with authentic relationships and events. Our children, our spouses, and our closest companions provide relationships in which deep meaning can be found because we care so deeply. We experience God's presence in those events and causes to which we have made a commitment. We seldom experience it in those circumstances that don't mean much anyway . . . but there are enough exceptions to that rule to keep us alert at all times.

The following essays are examples of what we mean— moments of truth that came unexpectedly, but left those who experienced them different people. There have undoubtedly been other "openings" in which God was speaking to us, and we just flat missed them or heard but didn't heed. Nevertheless, the moments that *are embraced* provide an essential ingredient in the life of faith. They remind us that God is alive and well and working in the world. God continues to speak to us as he did to men and women of old, of yesterday, and—yes—of today.

Ice Will Suffice

Background Information: While traveling on a speaking engagement in December, the author was snowbound in Kokomo, Indiana, for twenty-four hours. He was taken in, cared for, and his life was never in danger. Nonetheless, once was enough. Ice will suffice.

It is difficult for the weather of any season to live up to the poetry written about it. Snow, for example, viewed from inside a warm house after a hearty meal by a person who doesn't have to get a car started, is a beautiful sight. Photographers take pictures of it and publish them in *Ideals* magazine, and their white drifts warm our hearts. Snow, after all, makes our lawn look as good as our neighbor's, covering the bare spots and transforming the tricycle that didn't get put away into an art object.

Doubtless Whittier was warm and toasty when he wrote these lines in "Snowbound":

> What matter how the night behaved?
> What matter how the north wind raved?
> Blow high, blow low, not all its snow
> Could quench our hearth-fire's ruddy glow.

Outside, up to our armpits in drifts, we change our perspective dramatically. Indeed, our attitude toward snow is generally determined by what we plan to do that is hurt by it.

84

The snow that cancels school may also eliminate the trip to the movies. The person who claims that old-fashioned winters were tougher probably has a bad memory or a son who shovels the sidewalks.

Least appreciative of snow are those whose circumstances have placed them in cars on highways in the middle of senior-sized blizzards. True, their circumstances may be the result of human pride (i.e., plain cussedness), as some persons will challenge the weather, whether or not, simply because it is there. Others get trapped in blizzards because they forget that weather reports cannot *always* be depended upon to be wrong. Every now and then the weather reporter makes a mistake and guesses right, and travelers end up experiencing firsthand those television commercials warning against gas-line freeze and die-easy batteries.

Occasionally, of course, we deliberately venture into snowstorms because of emergencies, such as broken arms, a six-year-old's birthday party, or—if you live in Indiana—a high school basketball game. It is in such moments that one may change poets, moving from Whittier to Robert Frost. He tells us in "Fire and Ice" that, while "some say the world will end in fire" and "some say in ice . . . for destruction ice is also great and would suffice."

The deeper question, therefore, is this: is snow a metaphor for life? Whittier and Frost thought so, and we might, too, if we weren't otherwise preoccupied with shoveling, scraping, melting, or condemning it. Snow falls alike on the just and unjust, after which the just fall upon the snow the unjust failed to clear away. Into every life snow will fall, and some people will create sculpture out of it while others will make ice balls with rocks in them.

Life has its blizzards *and* its moments of quiet serenity by the fire. Both views are needed, for the person who knows only the blizzard may never be able to appreciate the beauty of a single snowflake. And armchair philosophers who have never experienced the rage of the storm are irrelevant.

Either view is incomplete without the other—a half-truth. And that, gentle readers, is the worst snow job of all.

Prayer: "O God, who controls nature, thank you for warm fires to greet us when we come in from the cold. In the name of him who once slept through a storm. Amen."

Term Paper 102

The course was called "Term Paper 102," a title promising as much excitement as watching the grass grow. Our high school junior daughter, Martha, chose to take it, however, because it would prepare her for college research papers.

The teacher turned out to be warmhearted but demanding. Each student could choose his or her own topic, but the finished paper was to take a position and document it fully. Martha decided to write on "The Historical Quaker Peace Testimony" for two reasons. (1) As a Friend she thought this would be a good opportunity to examine an important Quaker belief. (2) She was confident her teacher knew almost nothing about it, and her chances, therefore, of getting a good grade were proportionally increased.

Her research began with determination and high expectations. She developed a bibliography of which George Fox and William Penn themselves would have approved—particularly since a lot of their writings were included. She interviewed influential Friends who had been conscientious objectors, as well as some Quakers who had been involved in military service. She debated her position with the family and with Max, the leader of her youth group. Her research grew into an obsession, or as close to one as was possible for a seventeen-year-old with normal chromosomes.

In the process she became an evangelist for the Peace Testimony. No longer was the topic merely "interesting."

Not only did she want to earn a good grade, she now wished to convert her classmates into pacifists. It was a *right* belief to hold, she felt, not simply a nice idea to discuss.

The assignment required an oral report and then an open discussion of the paper's argument with the entire class. Martha looked forward to the encounter with a competitive spirit which clearly indicated the influence of her mother's Presbyterian genes. She anticipated questions and prepared her case with as much history, logic, and reason as she could muster.

Unfortunately, history, logic, and reason had little to do with the discussion. In trying out her ideas at home and in her youth group, she had always received a fair and usually sympathetic hearing. Those who had disagreed had been kind and friendly in their disagreements. The classroom encounter was something else.

Only three of her peers agreed with her. All others attacked both her arguments and her person: "Pacifists are just cowards. They're afraid to fight." She was smeared with guilt by association: "Your paper could have been written by a Commie!" Outnumbered badly by those who disagreed and battered by the passion of their arguments, Martha was literally reduced to tears. It was a bad day at Richmond High, one of the worst days of her seventeen-year-old life.

It was probably worse for her than it might have been for others in similar circumstances. Among our children Martha had always been the one most covetous of peer approval. I often teased her that she couldn't get dressed for school without a minimum of three phone calls to see what "everybody" was wearing that day. Then, too, she had invested herself in the idea, and it had become part of her view on life—part, as it were, of who she was.

All of her father's protective instincts surfaced when she shared the pain of the event with us. My impulse was to go and beat up all those kids who didn't believe in nonviolence!

The inconsistency of such a response was obvious, however, as there are times when one simply has to take her lumps and live to fight—or, in this case, to argue for *not* fighting—another day.

Two days later the impact of the experience became clearer. Martha, in discussing it with us, became quiet, deeply thoughtful, and pensive. After a moment she said, "You know, Mom and Dad, I guess what this whole thing shows me is that what *you* think—and what Max thinks—and what Mrs. Fuson thinks—is more important than what those kids think."

She had discovered that which Christians have been discovering for centuries. When we seek to do the will of God, we simultaneously choose a fellowship of persons with whom to share pain and joy. We move to a new level of maturity about what we believe and the cost of discipleship. It was a young girl's entrance into what Albert Schweitzer called "the fellowship of those who bear the mark of pain."

Paul might have had Martha's experience in mind when he wrote:

> Don't let the world around you squeeze you into its own mold, but let God remold your minds from within, so that you may prove in practice that the plan of God for you is good, meets all his demands and moves toward the goal of true maturity" (Rom. 12:2, Phillips).

Could Paul have taken Term Paper 102?

Strangers to
Our Best Selves

"There they were," Jim said, "three sweet, smiling, cherubic faces staring back at me through the rear window of a Pinto hatchback. I had pulled up on a line of traffic at a stoplight. My paternal instincts surged, and I smiled back at them, giving a small, friendly wave. Five or six years old. Pictures of innocence and life's goodness. What it could be and ought to be. Open. Trusting. Not yet hardened by life. Blue-eyed, flaxen-haired, with short, beribboned pigtails poking out behind each head. Clean and happy and friendly.

"I glanced at the light," he continued. "It was still red. I looked down again at the children in the window. They were still smiling, but now each was holding up one plump little hand with the middle finger extended in the classic obscene gesture. As the light changed and the traffic moved forward, the little girl in the middle—in case I had missed the point—repeated the gesture, more vigorously than before and with *both* hands.

"The honking of the car behind brought me back to reality, but I was still stunned and released the clutch too soon, stalling my car in the middle of traffic. This angered those behind me, and one man squealed around me, making loud references to my family tree."

Jim is a theologian and a good one. He is also the husband of one wife and the father of three children. As a result, he is no stranger to sin and its youthful manifestations. Still, his shock is our shock. After all, they were only five or six years old! I mean . . . really!

The incident reminds us, however, that small children are like adults. The double-edged experience at the stoplight was an enacted parable of life, showing the combination of goodness and sin *all* of us have. Jim didn't come *back* to reality after his initial surprise. What happened *was* reality.

We're both good *and* corrupt. Selfishness is a reality that has no age limitations. Pride is always present or hiding nearby. Accepting Christ as our personal Savior is an important act, but most of us who have done so will also admit that temptations to sin do not thereby automatically disappear. The reality is that cute children make obscene gestures. Presidents either admit to lust in their hearts or pretend it isn't there. Should Lady Godiva ride by, our puritan conscience tells us we'll be struck blind if we look. Most men, however, will risk at least one eye.

Middle-aged Christians ought not be surprised by this insight, but we often are. We're not surprised to discover sin in certain selected others—enemies, members of wrong political parties, or the spiritually mistaken. Their lives can be expected to exhibit corruption, insensitivity, lust for power, and bad breath. Our minds accept the fact that *all* have sinned, but major sins are generally attributed to others.

Sinfulness is not associated with small, blond children, nor with close friends and colleagues. Almost never is it attributed to loved ones or self. To the second group—*ours*— we attribute pardonable sins. Yet, avoiding neat divisions of *us* and *them* is a key to spiritual equanimity. Knowing that *our kind* will occasionally (if not regularly) exhibit pride, selfishness, insensitivity, and cussedness will take the shock out of the surprise when they are demonstrated.

Thus, we'll be better able to maintain our relationships when confronted by the bullheadedness of a colleague, the nastiness of a spouse, the slovenliness of a teenager, or our own secret spites. Spiritual equanimity comes when we discover that people don't have to be perfect to be cherished.

One teacher we know, who has remarkably warm and affectionate relationships with students and colleagues, shared his view of human nature: "I guess I don't expect a whole lot out of people. I don't necessarily expect my students to fail, but neither do I assume they'll do the right thing. When one of them promises with passionate commit-ment to get a term paper in on time and then doesn't, I don't experience anger or feel personally betrayed. I know human beings fail to meet commitments again and again. On the other hand, when a student *does* meet one of those commit-ments, I experience that which a *high* expectation denies— satisfaction and joy over something that otherwise would be taken for granted."

As a complete philosophy of life, such an attitude has its limitations. This writer's wife, while standing over our son in her ongoing efforts to motivate him to do his math, articulated an obvious critique: "If you don't expect much, you don't get much." Her point is valid, but it has its dangers, too. When we assume that people will shape up and they don't, our relationships are sometimes damaged.

This may explain why American parents are frequently estranged from their own children. The title of a recent article presents the dilemma: "Do Americans Dislike Chil-dren?" The article concluded that there is considerable evidence they do. And a cartoon in the same magazine helped explain why. The picture showed a small boy facing a distraught parent holding a report card that said the boy was an "underachiever." To this accusation the boy replied: "The problem is not that I'm an underachiever. The problem is that you're an overexpecter."

We do well, then, to allow room for the dark side of our natures. When we assume that *our* spouses, children, colleagues, and friends will necessarily measure up, we're setting ourselves up for disappointment and damaged relationships. We may find ourselves vaguely dissatisfied with those closest to us.

The manner in which we respond to human foibles reflects our view of humanity. Consider the variety of responses which might have been evoked had one of the three cherubs in the Pinto been our own:

1. "Ruthie would never have done that on her own. She'll not be allowed to play with Christie and Jo anymore. (Interpretation: "She didn't learn obscene gestures at our house, so we're not to blame." *Historical background:* "It was the snake's fault.")
2. "Ruthie has disgraced us all. I'm shocked and disappointed." (Interpretation: "It must be the chromosomes from her mother's side of the family." Biblical precedent: "The sins of the father are visited on the son, but the sins of the daughter embarrass the whole darn family.")
3. "Girls will be girls. It's no big deal." (Interpretation: "I once wrote dirty words on my teacher's windshield, and I turned out all right." Psychological device: "One person's sin is another's singularity.")

We may respond with a blend of all three responses, particularly when the reporter is Mrs. Jones, whom we've always thought was nosy anyhow. When we or those we love sin, we are tempted to blame outside forces. "The Devil—or bad companions or the world—made me do it." Or we let our pride turn it into a personal matter: "My own flesh and blood did this to me." Or we fail to take sin seriously: "Those who hear no evil, see no evil, nor speak no evil will never have much fun."

Once we've had time to deal with our emotions, however, a fourth response can become a live option:

4. "It's not all right to sin, but if we sin, it's all right." (Interpretation: "We don't want you to ride around town giving people—particularly theologians—the finger. That's wrong. But we love you, anyhow." Theological base: "God loves us, obscene gestures and all.")

That's good news. It's the Good News. It frees us from expecting perfection in others so that we can love them, and vice versa. And there's a lot of vice to versa. So much that only God through Christ could manage it.

On Thinking about My Wife and Realizing That We've Been Married Over 23 Years and Are Going to Stay That Way

Author's Note: In honor of my wife's forty-fifth birthday, this essay was written as a tribute—a birthday present, as it were. She was greatly surprised, especially since she wanted a new dress.

Dear Nancy:

In honor of your forty-fifth birthday and in the romantic spirit which has characterized our marriage, this chapter is dedicated to you. Ogden Nash has captured the event perfectly:

> Forty-five isn't really old, it's right on the border.
> At least, unless the elevator's out of order.

Reminders of aging are always near at hand. Life may begin at forty, but everything else starts to wear out, fall out, or spread out. Still, age doesn't really matter—unless you're made of cheese—and growing old is not so bad when one considers the alternative.

Your forty-fifth birthday means that several rich possibilities are now available to us that weren't ten, or even five, years ago:

—We've paid off the mortgage on our house. We've survived the "lien" years. Now, when our insurance payment is late, the company won't be able to intimidate us by telling the bank.

—With the two older children in college, we can walk right in and use the bathroom without standing outside the door pleading and pounding.

—The kids can worry about us for a change. Wasn't it touching when we were late getting home from our trip, and all four were pacing the floor! You nearly wept when Sarah said, "You could at least have called!"

The best realization of all that your birthday brings, however, is that we beat the odds. We've now spent more of our lives married than we've spent single. As other well-blessed couples can affirm, growing older is fine if we can do it together. Love may be blind and, yes, marriage is an eye-opener, but happily married people like what they see.

According to many researchers, we're supposed to be in the midlife crisis. Although writers about such things seldom interview people like you and me, the business executives, television performers, and other "pace-setters" who do get interviewed indicate we're not conforming statistically. I am supposed to flirt with, fantasize about, and possibly launch into a promiscuous phase during this period of my life, hoping to "cure fears, boredom, and a sudden sense of bodily decline."

Where did it all go right, Nancy? The fact that we're not pace-setters may have something to do with our having had a happy, solid marriage. After all, seductive women seldom throw themselves at gray-headed diabetics who teach religion in small, Quaker colleges. Then too, both of us promised a long time ago we wouldn't be unfaithful, and such promises—when kept—seriously inhibit wholehearted infidelity.

I know we're going to stay married until one of us dies, and this realization is a pleasant one. I'm sorry for those couples—and their name is legion—who "collide, crack up, or simply fall into the haphazard, slow-motion lapse known as the twenty-year marriage slump," as writer Gail Sheehy describes them. Maybe the pace-setters set too fast a pace, but I look forward to our remaining time together with anticipation, not resignation.

In fact, the anticipation we share makes the present interesting and the future tantalizing. You have invested yourself in children—our own and other people's—and life at our house continues to be an ongoing adventure. (By the way, who were those two boys you brought home from school for dinner last week?) Our own children have caught your spirit, and the grown-up ones don't give a hoot about being pace-setters. They want to save the world, preferably by Thursday, and everybody knows there's little money and less prestige in that.

Coincidence had a lot to do with our getting together, of course. And your being a really pretty woman didn't hurt, either, particularly since I could always see better than I could think. The key, however, has been our shared commitment. Antoine de Saint-Exupery's words could help many marriages if they were taken seriously:

> Love does not consist in gazing at each other but in looking outward in the same direction.

As we have shared values and faith, we've shared each other. Our cup overflows, and knowing that we drink from the same one—and clean up the spills together—brings contentment.

And joy.

Goin' Fishing

As we turned down the lane to my parents' home, a familiar tension gripped my shoulders and the usual lump settled in my throat. We were on our way to the Cincinnati Zoo to let the animals get a long look at our family, and we were depositing our infant daughter, Ruthie, with her grandparents for the day.

Leaving her was not the reason for my anxiety. Her grandparents adored Ruthie, and she basked in their adoration. Our other two daughters, Sarah and Martha, were also peaches in their grandparents' garden, living examples—in their opinion—that original sin might not apply in every instance, after all. When our oldest daughter, Sarah, had been born, my father had composed a poem and painstakingly burned its words onto a homemade plaque for her room. He had built, as a labor of love, a cradle for her, selecting each board and sanding every corner so that no splinter would prick her fingers.

When daughter Martha was born two years later, my father treated her as a priceless gift. Since we had moved within easy driving distance by that time, Martha actually enjoyed more "lap time," as Dad called it, than Sarah, and she wore out his pants legs crawling in and out of his lap. No grandparents could have been more affectionate or generous.

With Bret, however, it was different. Bret was adopted. He was interracial. He didn't fit. No matter that he was only three, wide-eyed, and adorable. He was an outsider, an intruder.

That's why dropping Ruthie at her grandparents produced familiar feelings of anxiety. Disagreement over the adoption had led to an estrangement that had never been experienced in all the years of growing up, graduating from college, getting married and having children. Everything I had done had been pleasing to my parents. I had been a dutiful child, and both Mother and Dad had made sacrifices so that their two sons could attend college and have opportunities they themselves had never enjoyed. In many ways my story was the model, middle-class, American saga—one generation helping the next to a better life.

My father and mother were waiting near the house as we drove up. Dad looked tired, and I felt old pangs of regret that this barrier stood between us—love for a boy he could only resent. The irony was that Dad had always wanted a grandson. While I had pleased him in most ways, I never had liked to do some of the things Dad enjoyed most, particularly fishing. Baiting hooks, bathing worms, and sitting on the side of a pond for hours while ants crawled into my socks was not my idea of fun on the farm. Dad had often shared hopes that one day a grandchild might appear on the scene and share the mystical significance of fishing. He had bought the acreage where he lived largely because it had a pond well-stocked with bass and bluegill.

As he walked slowly toward the car, limping slightly because of prostate trouble he had been having, I heard my voice barking at the children: "You kids stay in the car. We're just going to drop Ruthie off and then be on our way." They groaned but, for a change, obeyed without a fuss.

The instructions had a deeper meaning. They were the end result of an unspoken agreement between my parents and us. Bret's presence upset Dad, even though he couldn't articulate the reasons. It was the product of many years of unacknowledged but dormant prejudice carried over from his childhood. Mother, caught in the dual role of wife and parent, had tearfully delivered the message which had formalized the estrangement: "Tom, we think it better if Bret not come out to the house for a while."

Our response, born in anger and nurtured by pride, was to limit our visits; this denied them time with the other children. Bret, therefore, had not been on their property—even in the sanctity of the car—for many weeks.

When my parents visited our home . . . well, that was another matter. There was no attempt to keep grandfather and grandson apart and, given Bret's natural curiosity and magnetic attraction to the secret delights the pockets of grown-ups contained, segregation would have been impossible. Indeed, on those infrequent occasions when my father and my son found themselves together, there were tiny signs of mutual attraction, hints of comradery.

Certainly Bret was attracted to Dad. My father's pockets were a veritable gold mine of treasures to a three-year-old. Bret soon learned that they contained a knife, tape measure, coins, and unending supply of plastic ballpoint pens. He had charmed college students into numerous "horsy" rides, and many other grown-up visitors had smiled at his antics and rewarded him with attention. Why change his act for grandpa?

Bret assumed that people loved him, and he treated his adopted grandparents on the same premise. Some tokens of affection were reciprocated—a squeeze on the shoulder, a spontaneous smile at Bret's determined but doomed efforts to turn somersaults. As if embarrassed, Dad would catch himself and resume a posture of polite indifference. There were just enough hints to remind us of what could have been but, evidently, wasn't going to be.

On this day my father paused by the side of the car and gave a shy wave that was his trademark. All the children joined in a chorus of "hello"s and "hi, Grandad"s. Bret, as usual, sought extra attention. He leaned out his front-seat window and recited the greeting he had learned and invariably used over and over again on all living creatures: "How ya' doin', Grandad! How ya' doin'."

As Nancy got out to deliver Ruthie to her grandmother, Dad leaned against the car and peered in. "Hello, Sarah. Hello, Martha. . . . Hello, Bret. How ya' doin?"

Dad took Bret's hand and shook it. He felt his tiny biceps and challenged him to make it hard, to see how big a man he was getting to be, a ritual he had practiced on his own sons a hundred times.

Bret tightened his arm muscle as hard as he could, gritting his teeth with the effort. Finally, Dad spoke. He looked at Bret, but his words were for me. "You know, Bret, I was just saying to Grandma the other day . . . we haven't had ol' Bret out here for a long time. I bet he'd like to come out and go fishin' with me."

Dad died the following January. Before cancer took its toll, however, he and Bret fished together and walked in the woods and searched pockets for treasures. The real treasure, however, had already been found—love that brought healing and forgiveness to a father and his son.